CLB 1869
© 1993 CLB Publishing, Godalming, Surrey, England.
All rights reserved.
This edition published 1994 by Coombe Books.
Printed and bound in China
ISBN 0 86283 517 8

BEAUTIFUL
TORONTO

COOMBE BOOKS

It was April 27th, 1813, and Britain was at war with the United States of America. A small fleet of American ships was on its way to attack the town of York, capital of Upper Canada, as Ontario was then known, and an important naval yard. The outnumbered British troops tried to repel the attack, but by the end of the day the Americans were in control.

Virtually nothing remains of the York that fell to the Americans in 1813. Between the railway tracks and the highway, however, are the restored buildings of Old Fort York. It is now manned by staff in period costume who help recreate the life of an early-19th century garrison.

Since those early days increasingly large numbers of immigrants have found their way to Toronto, not only from within Canada but from around the globe. The population rapidly increased until it reached its present figure of some three million, turning Toronto into the bustling city of vitality we know today. Many of those immigrants brought with them their own cultures, lending colour and change to the city as a whole, and different outlooks on life spread throughout Toronto, so that it gradually changed its appellation from 'The Good', to 'People City'.

It is to this Toronto, the city of cosmopolitan tastes and mixed cultures, that the great landmarks and buildings belong. The CN Tower was completed in 1975 as part of a building boom that has transformed the city skyline in the last two decades. On three man-made islands off the shore of Lake Ontario has been constructed Ontario Place, the city's most important leisure complex, covering a total of 90 acres.

On the shore beside Ontario Place are the Exhibition Grounds. It is here that the Canadian National Exhibition is held each year. The Ex, as it is affectionately known, is billed as the largest annual exhibition in the world and anyone who has attended it will find that easy to believe. It is certainly one of the most exciting events and attracts participants and visitors from across the country and around the world. The Ex has been staged since 1879 and seems to grow bigger and better each year as new attractions take their place alongside established favourites.

Entertainment and interest can also be found in the various museums and galleries of the city. Toronto is rich in such attractions and counts itself fortunate that those responsible for the museums have decided that they should be fun, as well as interesting and educational. The Royal Ontario Museum is possibly the finest of the institutions. It has recently undergone extensive renovation and remodelling which has extended its facilities to include such innovations as a toy-and-snack shop for children. The fun aspect of the museum does not, however, detract from its main purpose; it does, after all, house some 5,000,000 exhibits!

A short distance from the museum stands Yorkville. This area of Victorian houses and bricked-over sidewalks was once a rather disreputable section of the city before the massive renovation scheme got under way. Whilst keeping the original buildings around Yorkville Avenue, the developers smartened up the district and chic boutiques and fine restaurants soon opened, where the fashionable of the city could shop and dine. The scheme was most successful and Yorkville is now one of the places all visitors are recommended to visit.

From the isolated, backwoods capital of York, which the Americans sacked so many years ago, Toronto has matured into a dynamic, cosmopolitan city which, whilst honouring its past, has its eye fixed firmly on the future.

Facing page: Toronto's striking CN Tower, a dramatic contrast to the surrounding city.

The statue of Sir John A. Macdonald (below), first prime minister of Canada, faces the imposing headquarters of Ontario Hydro by Queen's Park. Bottom: Royal Bank Plaza's garden court, and (right) snow-covered Nathan Phillips Square, illuminated at night.

Previous pages: (left) St. James Anglican Cathedral, and (right) Old City Hall. Right: Chinatown's Dundas Street, (far right) a pipe band in Nathan Phillips Square, (below) a café in Yorkville, and (bottom) Toronto Islands.

Left: Royal Bank Plaza's glass tower, in downtown Toronto (above). Far left: city girls enjoying a chat. Top right: the turrets of Holy Trinity Church behind the graceful curve of Roy Thomson Hall, and (right) Toronto Inner Harbour.

Toronto, with its entertainment complex of space-age buildings at Ontario Place (far right) and the fun and excitement to be found in Canada's Wonderland (remaining pictures), offers a superb range of leisure-time activities.

Below and far left centre: Canada's Wonderland theme park at Vaughan. Left and far left: picnic area, and (bottom) pony rides, on leafy Toronto Islands. Bottom left: the grassy slopes of the Children's Village, Ontario Place.

Facing page: (bottom left) a tram in Dundas Street, (top left) relaxing in the grounds of the Toronto Dominion Centre and (centre left) at a streetside Yorkville café, and (right) a craftware exhibition in Nathan Phillips Square. Above: a sundial, backed by City Hall, and (left) Toronto Harbour.

Ontario Place (top), with its Children's Village (above), and the parkland of Toronto Islands (remaining pictures) are two of Toronto's most popular recreation areas.

Left and far left centre: an art display near Nathan Phillips Square. Far left: Hazelton Café, (bottom left) Fenton's Restaurant, and (below) a Yorkville café. Bottom: striking sculpture by Henry Moore.

Art Gallery of Ontario

Yonge Street (bottom), on which both Eatons and Simpsons are situated, is one of the best-known streets in Canada. Remaining pictures: fresh fish, fruit, and vegetables at Kensington Market.

Left: visitors relax among the outdoor exhibits (above and top) in Nathan Phillips Square. Top left: the illuminated Cinesphere at Ontario Place, and (far left) the Council Chamber of City Hall.

Above and top right: the fine interior of St. James Anglican Cathedral. The Grange (right and far right), an elegant Georgian house, was constructed in 1817 and was the first home of the Art Gallery of Ontario.

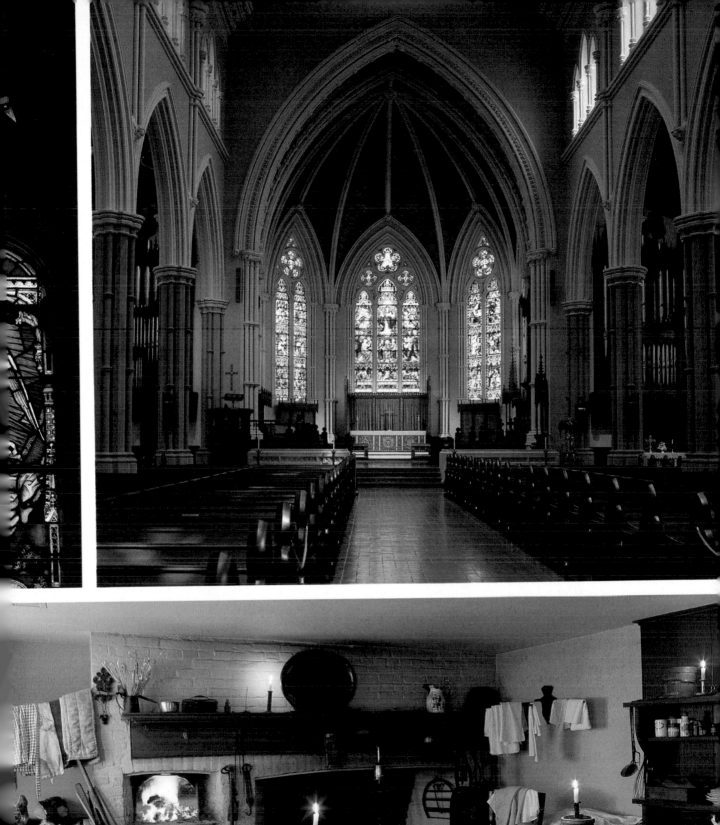

Among Toronto's most impressive modern buildings are the Eaton Centre shopping complex (bottom and facing page), which utilises natural lighting, glass and greenery to good effect, and Hydro Place (right). Equally striking are the rounded dome of the sports stadium and the CN Tower (overleaf). Below: a city lunch break.

The magnificent Eaton Centre (these pages), standing on Yonge Street, extends over several blocks of central Toronto and houses over 300 fine shops, stores and restaurants on three levels, all enclosed by an arched glass roof.

The Toronto Islands Ferry (facing page top) departs from the foot of Yonge Street (left), one of the busiest thoroughfares in the city. Below and facing page bottom: the Ice Canoe Race, which forms such a central feature of Winterfest.

Beyond the city centre stands grand, Gothic Casa Loma (left), built by Sir Henry Pellatt before the First World War. Old Fort York (above and top), with its costumed staff, guards the city's historic waterfront area.

Above: Nathan Phillips
Square, (right) the CN
Tower, and (top) University
Avenue. Facing page: (top)
Yonge Street, and (bottom)
the Provincial Parliament
Buildings.

Black Creek Pioneer Village (these pages) is a recreated mid-19th-century Ontario village where costumed staff re-enact the lifestyle of former days. Overleaf: (left) the ferry between the mainland and Toronto Islands (right).

Bottom: a city shop owner enjoys the summer air. Right and facing page: the modern, starkly beautiful City Hall, designed by Viljo Revell.

Bottom: the reflecting glass wall of the Ontario Hydro building. Far left: swan boats on leafy Toronto Islands. The exhilarating theme park of Canada's Wonderland (remaining pictures) was opened in 1981, and stands in Vaughan, some 20 miles north of the city. Overleaf: the beautiful Blue Mountain Ski Resort, also north of Toronto.

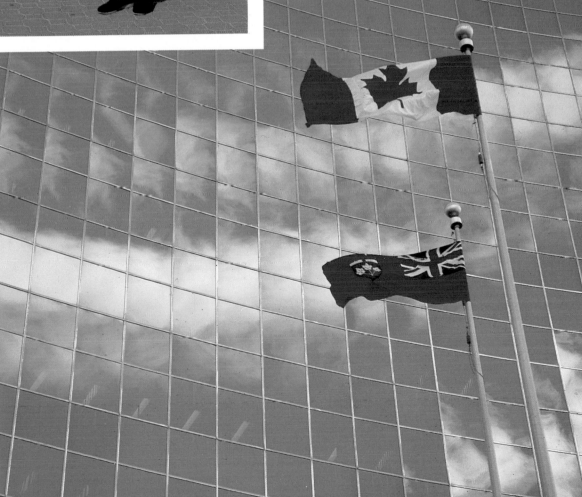

Glimpsed between the
buildings on Nathan Phillips
Square (above), high above
the domed sports stadium
(facing page), or from the
waters of Lake Ontario
(overleaf), the CN Tower is
truly Toronto's most
spectacular landmark. Right:
city silhouettes.

Ontario Place (far right), with its dome-shaped Cinesphere, lies on the city's waterfront. Above: yachts moored near the city's harbour, and (below and right) pleasant Toronto Islands.

Ontario Place (left) is based on the concept of the Tivoli Gardens in Copenhagen and includes the Children's Village (above). Below: Canada's Wonderland.